PUFFI

Plotting a
Tudors and Stuar

Scoular Anderson studied graphic design at the Glasgow School of Art. He then worked as an illustrator for London University and as a teacher in a large comprehensive school in central Scotland. He began illustrating and writing, for both children and adults, after leaving art school. He has returned to his native Argyllshire in the west of Scotland, where he works freelance.

Some other books by Scoular Anderson

Fiction

THE CURSE OF HACKJAW ISLAND

Non-fiction

LAND AHOY! THE STORY OF CHRISTOPHER
    COLUMBUS
A PLUNDER OF PIRATES
THE PUFFIN FACT FILE OF KINGS AND QUEENS
PUZZLING PEOPLE
RAIDING AND TRADING: VIKINGS WITH A FEW
    GORY BITS

Large format books

PROJECT COLUMBUS
PROJECT PIRATES

Scoular Anderson

Plotting and Chopping

Tudors and Stuarts
With a Few Gory Bits

PUFFIN BOOKS

PUFFIN BOOKS

Published by the Penguin Group
Penguin Books Ltd, 27 Wrights Lane, London W8 5TZ, England
Penguin Books USA Inc., 375 Hudson Street, New York, New York 10014, USA
Penguin Books Australia Ltd, Ringwood, Victoria, Australia
Penguin Books Canada Ltd, 10 Alcorn Avenue, Toronto, Ontario, Canada M4V 3B2
Penguin Books (NZ) Ltd, 182–190 Wairau Road, Auckland 10, New Zealand

Penguin Books Ltd, Registered Offices: Harmondsworth, Middlesex, England

First published 1995
1 3 5 7 9 10 8 6 4 2

Copyright © Scoular Anderson, 1995
All rights reserved

The moral right of the author/illustrator has been asserted

Typeset by RefineCatch Ltd, Bungay, Suffolk
Set in Monophoto Bembo

Printed in England by Clays Ltd, St Ives plc

Except in the United States of America, this book is sold subject
to the condition that it shall not, by way of trade or otherwise, be lent,
re-sold, hired out, or otherwise circulated without the publisher's
prior consent in any form of binding or cover other than that in
which it is published and without a similar condition including this
condition being imposed on the subsequent purchaser

British Library Cataloguing in Publication Data
A CIP catalogue record for this book is available
from the British Library

ISBN 0 140 37138 9

CONTENTS

Tudors and Stuarts Family Tree	6
The Tudors	8
Making Progress	10
Henry VII	14
How to Pass the Time	16
Henry VIII	18
The Wives of Henry VIII	20
Down Come the Monasteries	22
Closing In and Shutting Out	24
England and Other Nations	24
The Great Harry	26
Tudor Soldiers	28
Where They Lived	30
Edward VI	32
Furniture	34
A Healthy Appetite	36
Mary I	38
Travelling Around	40
Elizabeth I	42
Elizabeth and Mary Queen of Scots	44
Sailors and Explorers	46
Armada!	48
Fashion	50
Art Facts	52
The Stuarts	54
James VI and I	58
Remember! Remember! The Fifth of November	60
Travel	62
At School and at Play	64
Charles I	66
The Civil War	68
Foody subjects	72
Charles II	74
Science	76
Disease and Disaster	78
Buildings	80
James II	82
Fashion	84
William III and Mary II	86
Outside and In	88
Anne	90
Art Facts	92
Index	94

TUDORS and STUARTS
Family Tree

TUDORS

HENRY VII

HENRY VIII

EDWARD VI

MARY I

ELIZABETH I

STUARTS

MARGARET *married* JAMES IV OF SCOTLAND

JAMES V OF SCOTLAND

MARY QUEEN of SCOTS

JAMES VI and I

CHARLES I

CHARLES II   MARY

JAMES II

MARY II & WILLIAM III

JAMES

BONNIE PRINCE CHARLIE   ANNE

THE TUDORS

Tudor kings and queens ran the country from their palaces. They had many advisers but the monarch usually made the final decision; for instance, how to spend money, when to go to war, which courtiers should be shown favours, who should be dismissed or executed.

There was a parliament but it was not like the one we have today. Parliament met every now and then to discuss things which involved ordinary people, like taxes.

During the 118 years of the Tudors, Parliament met for only eight of those years!

THE ROYAL COURT WAS A PLACE NOT ONLY OF BUSINESS BUT OF SCANDAL, JEALOUSY, GOSSIP, RUMOURS, PLOTS ETC.

The Tudor kings and queens were expected to set an example in religious beliefs. Whatever religion the monarch chose, the people were expected to follow.

Up until the reign of Henry VII, the country had been Catholic. However, the new Protestant religion was spreading quickly through Europe.

This caused all sorts of problems as one monarch had a different religion from the next, and people began to choose a religion which was different from the monarch's.

MAKING PROGRESS

The Tudor monarchs often went on trips called Progresses. That meant horses and carts being piled high with royal luggage. Furniture, including beds, went too. The monarch would then travel round the country, staying at the houses of rich favourites.

Progress was slow because of the number of courtiers, servants, guards and so on who travelled as well.

There were several reasons why the monarch went on a Progress:

REASON 1

It saved royal money. The rich nobles had to feed their guests, the monarch and the court, sometimes for several weeks. This was a strain on the host, of course – but think of the honour!

REASON 2

Plumbing wasn't very good in the royal palaces. It could get very smelly, especially in summer. Things could be freshened up if the buildings were left empty for a month or two.

REASON 3

Ordinary people could catch a glimpse of the king or queen. It was very important for the power and the glory of the monarch to be seen by all. Queen Elizabeth I liked to go on walkabouts so she could talk to the locals.

When a monarch arrived in town there would be great celebrations with speeches, flags and fireworks.

HENRY VII
1485 ~ 1509

England had been troubled for over thirty years by a civil war. It was known as the Wars of the Roses. The war was really a fierce argument about who was the rightful king of England.

All this ended when Henry VII became king. He belonged to a Welsh family called Tewdwr. The name was written in English as Tudor.

His claim to the throne was a pretty flimsy one but he had some royal blood in his veins.

He defeated Richard III at the Battle of Bosworth and became the first Tudor monarch.

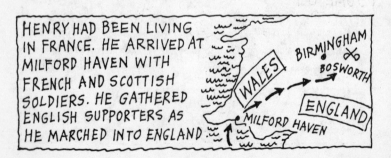

HENRY HAD BEEN LIVING IN FRANCE. HE ARRIVED AT MILFORD HAVEN WITH FRENCH AND SCOTTISH SOLDIERS. HE GATHERED ENGLISH SUPPORTERS AS HE MARCHED INTO ENGLAND

WALES
BIRMINGHAM
BOSWORTH
ENGLAND
MILFORD HAVEN

Henry was a clever and efficient ruler, firm but not cruel. He brought peace to the country after years of fighting.

He made peace with England's enemies, the French and the Scots. His daughter married the King of Scotland.

People complained that his taxes were too high, but he wasn't a spendthrift. When he died the treasury was full – but his son was soon going to empty it when he became king!

HENRY HAD MANY ENEMIES IN THE COUNTRY. VARIOUS PLOTS WERE MADE AGAINST HIM. SOME REBELS CLAIMED A 10-YEAR-OLD BOY CALLED LAMBERT SIMNEL WAS THE SON OF EDWARD IV. HE WAS THEREFORE THE RIGHTFUL KING.

SOME OTHERS CLAIMED THAT A FRENCH LAD CALLED PERKIN WARBECK WAS ALSO THE SON OF A KING OF ENGLAND.

NONE OF THESE PLOTS WAS SUCCESSFUL.

HOW TO PASS THE TIME

ORDINARY PEOPLE DIDN'T HAVE MUCH FREE TIME. THEY WERE EXPECTED TO WORK FROM DAWN TO DUSK, SIX DAYS A WEEK. THEY STILL FOUND TIME FOR SPORT, EVEN THOUGH IT WAS ILLEGAL FOR THEM TO PLAY CERTAIN GAMES.

CROSSBOWS WERE BECOMING SO POPULAR THAT LONGBOW-MAKERS WERE LOSING TRADE. (SOME WERE GOING OFF TO FIND WORK IN ENEMY SCOTLAND.) CROSSBOWS WERE EVENTUALLY BANNED ALONG WITH VARIOUS OTHER SPORTS.

> • PERSONS NOT OF NOBLE BIRTH MUST <u>NOT</u> PLAY: TENNIS
> BOWLS
> SKITTLES
> DICE
> CARDS
> ON PAIN OF IMPRISONMENT

ARCHERY WAS POPULAR. MEN WERE EXPECTED TO PRACTISE REGULARLY AT THE BUTTS IN CASE THEY WERE NEEDED TO DEFEND THE COUNTRY.

FOOTBALL WAS A FAVOURITE SPORT WITH YOUNG MEN (AND WOMEN). IT WAS A ROUGH GAME. SOMETIMES THE GOALMOUTHS COULD BE 3 MILES APART!

THE NOBLES HELD TOURNAMENTS WHERE ARMOURED KNIGHTS JOUSTED WITH EACH OTHER.

HUNTING WAS A FAVOURITE SPORT OF KINGS AND QUEENS. IN WINTER, WHEN THEY DIDN'T HUNT, THEY WOULD GO HAWKING.

TENNIS WAS POPULAR AT THE PALACE AND WAS PLAYED ON AN INDOOR COURT.

THERE WERE SPECIAL PITS FOR BEAR-BAITING. IT WAS A CRUEL SPORT BUT ONE OF QUEEN ELIZABETH'S FAVOURITES.

IN QUEEN ELIZABETH'S TIME YOU COULD JUST RELAX IN AN INN, OF COURSE, AND SMOKE A PIPE OF THE NEWLY DISCOVERED TOBACCO.

17

HENRY VIII
1509~1547

Henry was an energetic man. During the day he liked to hunt or joust or practise archery. He danced or played music in the evening. He often played cards well into the night and had a huge appetite for food and drink.

This didn't leave much time for official business. Although he met his advisers before and after supper, Henry was content to let other people run the country.

Cardinal Wolsey and Thomas Cromwell were two of those men. They both became very powerful. Cardinal Wolsey's wealth and magnificent palaces almost outshone the king's.

Cardinal Wolsey

Thomas Cromwell

But, in the end, both men got on the wrong side of their master. Henry dismissed Wolsey and confiscated his property. He had Cromwell executed.

THE WIVES OF HENRY VIII

Henry wanted a son as a future king. It was thought that a daughter wouldn't be able to control the country if she became queen.

However, his first wife, Catherine of Aragon, produced a daughter, Mary. Henry decided to divorce Catherine, but the Pope said it would not be allowed.

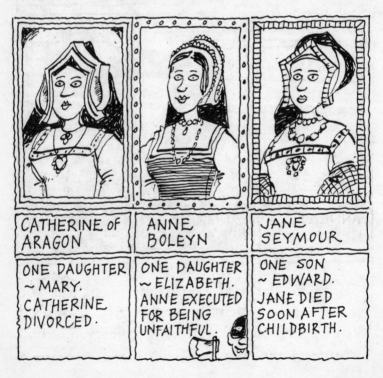

CATHERINE of ARAGON	ANNE BOLEYN	JANE SEYMOUR
ONE DAUGHTER ~ MARY. CATHERINE DIVORCED.	ONE DAUGHTER ~ ELIZABETH. ANNE EXECUTED FOR BEING UNFAITHFUL.	ONE SON ~ EDWARD. JANE DIED SOON AFTER CHILDBIRTH.

Henry was arrogant and short-tempered. He liked to have things his own way. When Cardinal Wolsey failed to get the king a divorce, he was dismissed. Henry then proclaimed himself the Supreme Head of the Church of England. In other words, the Pope was no longer in charge of the English Church. Henry could now grant himself a divorce.

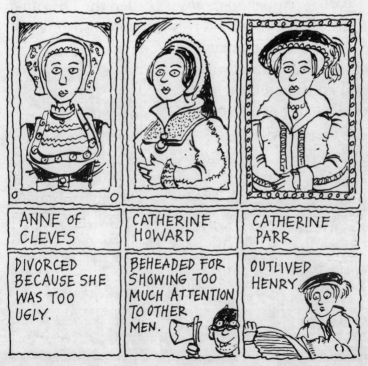

ANNE OF CLEVES	CATHERINE HOWARD	CATHERINE PARR
DIVORCED BECAUSE SHE WAS TOO UGLY.	BEHEADED FOR SHOWING TOO MUCH ATTENTION TO OTHER MEN.	OUTLIVED HENRY.

DOWN COME THE MONASTERIES

People were getting fed up with the way churchmen lived and behaved. Monks and bishops were becoming lazy and many didn't carry out their duties.

Some had become very rich. They owned huge estates, houses, farms, even coal-mines. Now that Henry was Supreme Head of the Church, he decided to tidy things up.

What happened next was called the Dissolution of the Monasteries (dissolution means breaking up). Henry closed the monasteries and confiscated their wealth and property.

THE VALUABLE LEAD WAS STRIPPED FROM THE ROOFS SO THEY QUICKLY FELL INTO RUIN.

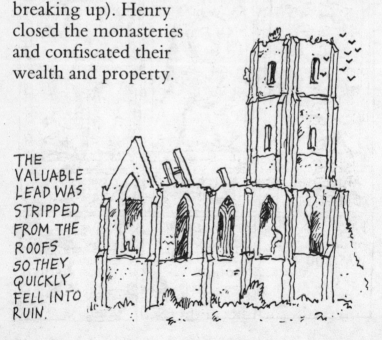

Henry gave away some of the church estates to court favourites. Other people bought property at knock-down prices.

One gentleman received unusual payment when he won a gambling game with the king . . .

Not all monks were lazy and many monasteries supplied worthwhile services. They gave food to beggars and the poor. They acted as hospitals and schools. Travellers would be given a bed for the night if there wasn't an inn nearby.

All this was now gone. It took some time for Parliament to set up charities which would feed the poor and schools which would educate the children.

CLOSING IN AND SHUTTING OUT

Wool and cloth were the things England sold abroad. Landowners began to enclose land with fences so they could keep more sheep. This meant that poorer folk lost their farm plots. As sheep didn't need much looking after, many farm-hands lost their jobs.

ENGLAND AND OTHER NATIONS

To the English, Wales was a wild, lawless place, but an Act of Union was signed during Henry's reign. The Welsh were given equal rights in England and could send their MPs to the parliament at Westminster. In return, Wales was divided up into counties and given an English system of government.

Henry had trouble with two of England's old enemies – the French and the Scots. (They were always ganging up together against the English.)

An English army defeated the Scots at the Battle of Flodden. The Scottish king was killed along with many of his nobles.

In the Middle Ages England owned large parts of France. By Henry's time there was only a little bit of this territory left. Henry and the French king had many skirmishes over this land.

They once met for peace talks where they tried to outdo each other with magnificent display. The place was called the Field of Cloth-of-Gold because of the richly decorated marquees each king put up.

They were soon at war again!

HENRY FOUNDED THE
ROYAL NAVY. HE HAD
MANY SHIPS BUILT (RATHER
THAN HIRING THEM FROM
OTHERS).
THE 'GREAT HARRY' WAS
ONE OF HENRY'S SHIPS.
HE ORDERED THE
SHIPYARD TO "BUILD
A SHIP THE LIKE OF
WHICH ENGLAND HAS
NEVER SEEN".
THE SIDES OF THE
SHIP WERE RICHLY
PAINTED.

IT CARRIED 700 CREW.
301 WERE SAILORS,
50 WERE GUNNERS AND
349 WERE SOLDIERS.
THE SHIP HAD 122
CANNONS.

26

The Great Harry

TUDOR SOLDIERS

THE TUDORS DIDN'T HAVE A PERMANENT ARMY. WHEN THE MONARCH WANTED TO GO TO WAR EACH NOBLE AND GENTLEMAN WAS EXPECTED TO SUPPLY SOME MEN AND WEAPONS.

SOMETIMES MERCENARIES (PAID SOLDIERS) WERE HIRED FROM ABROAD. THERE WAS ALSO A GROUP OF MEN KNOWN AS 'CRACKERS' WHO FOUGHT IN RETURN FOR LOOT GATHERED ON THE BATTLEFIELD.

AS YOU CAN IMAGINE FROM THIS COLLECTION OF MEN, THE FIGHTING FORCE WAS NOT VERY WELL DISCIPLINED.

LONGBOWMAN

SKILLED ENGLISH LONGBOWMEN HAD WON MANY BATTLES IN THE PAST. THEY WERE STILL USED BY THE TUDORS EVEN THOUGH THEIR WEAPON WERE BECOMIN OLD-FASHIONE

BILLMAN →

A BILL

PADDED JACKET →

SOLDIERS DIDN'T WEAR MUCH ARMOUR - PERHAPS JUST A BREASTPLATE SOME CHAIN-MAIL AND A HELMET.

28

NOBLES STILL WORE FULL ARMOUR WHEN ON HORSEBACK BUT THE ENGLISH HAD GREAT DIFFICULTY IN FINDING HORSES STRONG ENOUGH FOR THE TASK.

ARQUEBUSIER
(AN ARQUEBUS WAS A TYPE OF GUN.)

GUNS AND PISTOLS WERE BECOMING POPULAR BUT THEY WERE STILL VERY SLOW TO FIRE AND COULDN'T BE USED IN THE RAIN.
(WET GUNPOWDER!)

YEOMEN OF THE GUARD

THE MONARCH HAD A BAND OF ABOUT 100 YEOMEN OF THE GUARD FOR PERSONAL PROTECTION.
(STILL AROUND TODAY AS 'BEEFEATERS' IN THE TOWER OF LONDON!)

WHERE THEY LIVED

UP UNTIL THIS TIME, CITIES AND TOWNS WERE
SURROUNDED BY A WALL FOR PROTECTION. NOBLES
LIVED IN CASTLES.
NOW THE COUNTRY WAS BECOMING MORE PEACEFUL.
AS CITY WALLS WERE NOT NEEDED, PEOPLE TOOK
THE STONES TO BUILD HOUSES. CASTLES FELL INTO
RUIN. IN ANY CASE, CASTLES AND WALLS WERE NO
PROTECTION AGAINST THE NEW CANNONS.

PEACE BROUGHT
PROSPERITY AND
THE NOBLES AND
MERCHANTS
BEGAN TO BUILD
MORE COMFORTABLE
HOUSES.
HOUSES WERE
BUILT OF A WOODEN
FRAME FILLED
WITH WATTLE (TWIGS)
AND COVERED IN
PLASTER.

MORE HOUSES
WERE BEING
BUILT OF STONE
OR THE LATEST
MATERIAL – BRICK.

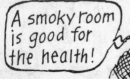

A smoky room is good for the health!

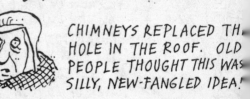

CHIMNEYS REPLACED TH
HOLE IN THE ROOF. OLD
PEOPLE THOUGHT THIS WAS
SILLY, NEW-FANGLED IDEA!

BETTER-QUALITY GLASS WAS BEING
MANUFACTURED. WINDOWS BECAME
LARGER. ORDINARY FOLK COULDN'T
AFFORD MUCH GLASS. SOMETIMES THEIR
WINDOWS WERE ONLY HALF-GLAZED,
WITH WOODEN DOORS IN THE OTHER HALF.

POOR COUNTRY FOLK LIVED IN HOUSES
WITH ONE STOREY, TWO ROOMS AND
A MUD FLOOR.

IN THE COUNTRY
HOUSES WERE
BUILT BY LOCAL
CRAFTSMEN. RICH
PEOPLE WOULD
PROBABLY HAVE
USED ONE OF
THE BIG BUILDING
COMPANIES THAT
WERE SPRINGING
UP.

IN TOWNS AND
CITIES BUILDINGS
WERE CRAMMED
TOGETHER ALONG
NARROW STREETS.

31

Edward was only ten when his father died. On his deathbed, Henry VIII chose Edward Seymour as Protector of the kingdom until Edward was old enough to rule on his own.

Within a few weeks, Edward Seymour gave himself the title of Duke of Somerset. He was soon pushed out of the way by the Duke of Northumberland. (He had Somerset executed.)

England was now officially a Protestant country and both Edward and Northumberland wanted it to remain like that.

However, Edward was a sickly boy and didn't look as if he would live long. His half-sister, Mary, would be the next queen and she was a Catholic.

Northumberland persuaded Edward to

choose Lady Jane Grey as the next queen. (She was a distant relative.) But Mary had many supporters, and when Edward died at the age of sixteen, she was proclaimed queen. Both Northumberland and Lady Jane Grey were executed.

During Henry VIII's reign, a man called William Tyndale translated the Bible into English. Until this time, bibles were written in Latin and only priests and well-educated people could read them. Tyndale said:

I want even the ploughboy to understand the Bible as well as you.

However, he had to have his Bible printed abroad. It was outlawed in England. Churchmen thought that it was their job to read the Bible and ordinary people should not be allowed to do so.

Bibles had to be smuggled into the country in bales of straw until Edward eventually allowed bibles to be read in English.

FURNITURE

FURNITURE BECAME MORE COMFORTABLE AND MORE DECORATIVE DURING THE TUDOR AGE. CHAIRS, TABLES, BEDS AND CUPBOARDS HAD CARVED PATTERNS ON THEM. THERE WERE NO CARPETS ON THE FLOORS AND YOU WOULDN'T FIND MANY COMFY CUSHIONS!

THERE WERE MATTRESSES AND PILLOWS ON THE BEDS BUT MOST CHAIRS WERE NOT UPHOLSTERED. THERE WERE CUPBOARDS FOR JUST ABOUT EVERYTHING - FOOD, BLANKETS, DISHES ETC.

THE HOUSES OF POOR PEOPLE STILL HAD EARTH FLOORS. STOOLS AND CHAIRS WITH THREE LEGS DIDN'T WOBBLE SO MUCH ON AN UNEVEN SURFACE.

THERE WERE FOUR-POSTER
BEDS WITH CURTAINS TO
PULL AROUND. THEY KEPT OUT
THE DRAUGHTS AND GAVE
SOME PRIVACY. THERE
WERE NO CORRIDORS IN
TUDOR HOUSES AND
PEOPLE HAD TO WALK
THROUGH ONE ROOM TO GET
TO THE NEXT.
SOME HOUSES ONLY HAD ONE
BED SO THE WHOLE FAMILY
SLEPT TOGETHER. YOU MIGHT
HAVE TO SHARE A BED WITH
STRANGERS AT AN INN!

A HEALTHY APPETITE

FOREIGN VISITORS OFTEN REMARKED ON THE LARGE AMOUNT OF FOOD THE ENGLISH ATE.

ON SPECIAL OCCASIONS AT COURT, THERE WERE BANQUETS. ALL SORTS OF MAGNIFICENT DISHES WERE SERVED: ROAST PEACOCKS, ENORMOUS PIES, SWEETMEATS CARVED INTO FANTASTIC SHAPES.

TUDOR MENU

Beef, mutton, chickens, pigeons, venison, bread, butter, cheese, eggs, fish, puddings, pastries, pies, biscuits and lots of honey!

EVEN ORDINARY PEOPLE ATE WELL. IN THE COUNTR[Y] THEY GREW MOST OF THEIR OWN FOOD. THERE WERE RABBITS TO TRAP AND CHICKENS IN THEIR YARDS. IN TOWNS THERE WERE COOKSHOPS, SORTS OF TUDO[R] TAKE-AWAYS, WHERE YOU COULD BUY HOT FOOD OR YOU COULD TAKE YOUR OWN FOOD TO BE COOKED.

ALL COOKING WAS DONE OVER AN OPEN FIRE, WHETHER IT WAS IN A PEASANT'S COTTAGE OR A ROYA[L] PALACE. ABOUT 1,500 PEOPLE HAD TO BE FED IN THE PALACE EACH DAY!

36

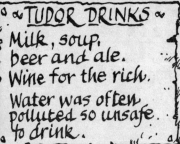

TUDOR DRINKS

Milk, soup,
beer and ale.
Wine for the rich.
Water was often
polluted so unsafe
to drink.

AFTER THE DISCOVERY OF
THE AMERICAS BY COLUMBUS
IN 1492, NEW FOODS BEGAN
TO ARRIVE IN ENGLAND:
POTATOES and TOMATOES
FROM SOUTH AMERICA,
TURKEY FROM CENTRAL
AMERICA, SUGAR FROM THE
WEST INDIES.

THERE WERE
FRUIT AND
VEGETABLES
OF ALL KINDS
BUT PEOPLE
THOUGHT THAT
EATING THEM RAW WAS BAD
FOR YOU.

raw apple, yuk!

TOO MANY SWEET THINGS
TURNED PEOPLE'S TEETH
BLACK. THEY
COULD HAVE
THEM SCRAPED
AND BLEACHED
WITH ACID —
A DODGY
REMEDY!

ORDINARY FOLK ATE FROM
WOODEN PLATES. THEY HAD
CUPS AND SPOONS OF HORN.
THERE WAS LIKELY TO BE ONLY
ONE KNIFE IN THE HOUSE.

WEALTHIER HOUSEHOLDS
MIGHT HAVE
CUPS AND
PLATES OF
PEWTER
(A KIND OF
METAL).

THE RICH WERE PROUD OF
THEIR GOLD AND SILVER
TABLEWARE. WINE GLASSES
HAD JUST ARRIVED FROM
ITALY. FORKS WERE STILL
A NOVELTY — EVEN FOR THE
KING — EVERYONE USED THEIR
FINGERS.

It'll never catch on!

37

MARY
1553 ~ 1558
I

Mary's short reign was a disaster.

Her father had treated her as a nobody. She had been dismissed from court and separated from her mother. She became an unhappy woman, out of touch with the world.

At first people welcomed her as queen, but before long she was very unpopular because she made some dreadful decisions.

She decided to marry the king of Spain, but the English didn't want to become part of Spain. Besides, Spain was a Catholic

MARY- 37 YEARS OLD - BUT LOOKED OLDER - A BIT FLABBY - BADLY DRESSED.

PHILIP - 26 YEARS OLD — COLD AND HAUGHTY.

HE SOON LEFT HER AND RETURNED TO SPAIN.

country. Mary was also a Catholic and she wanted to turn England back into a Catholic country.

People began to protest. Sir Thomas Wyatt arrived at the gates of London at the head of a protest march of 3,000 people.

SOME PROTESTERS MANAGED TO GET INTO THE PALACE BRINGING A DOG WITH ITS HEAD SHAVED LIKE A PRIEST.

Mary's next decision earned her the title of 'Bloody Mary'. She decided to burn at the stake people who claimed they were Protestants. She started with several archbishops, followed by almost three hundred people.

BURNING AT THE STAKE WAS A SLOW, CRUEL DEATH. SMOKE OFTEN KILLED VICTIMS BEFORE THE FLAMES DID. FRIENDS THREW EXTRA FAGGOTS ON THE FIRE TO MAKE IT BURN QUICKER AND HASTEN DEATH.

Spain persuaded England to join in a war against France. Just before Mary's death, the French captured the town of Calais. This was the last little bit of the huge area of France which England once owned.

TRAVELLING AROUND

THERE WERE FOUR MAIN ROADS ACROSS THE COUNTRY. THEY WERE KEPT IN FAIRLY GOOD CONDITION BECAUSE THEY WERE USED BY IMPORTANT PEOPLE AND MESSENGERS.

OTHER ROADS WERE USUALLY VERY MUDDY AND FULL OF POTHOLES. MOST PEOPLE TRAVELLED BY HORSE. COACHES WERE A NEW IDEA WHICH HADN'T YET CAUGHT ON. THEY WERE VERY UNCOMFORTABLE BECAUSE THEY HAD NO SPRINGS.

IT WAS SAFER TO TRAVEL WITH OTHERS AS PROTECTION AGAINST HIGHWAYMEN AND 'MOSSTROOPERS'

SCOTLAND

EDINBURGH
BERWICK-UPON-TWEED

ENGLAND

IRELAND

WALES
·CHESTER

PLYMOUTH
LONDON·
DOVER·
FRANCE

TRAVELLERS COULD HIRE R EXCHANGE HORSES AT N INN. THE INNS WERE ERY COMFORTABLE. OMETIMES THE FRIENDLY, ELPFUL SERVICE HAD REASON. SOME INN-EEPERS PASSED ON EFUL INFORMATION TO GHWAYMEN.

Says he's going to Norwich ...two nice, heavy bags... leaving in the morning...

OOH! OUCH!

A TUDOR COACH

WATER TRANSPORT – EITHER BY SEA OR BY RIVER – WAS THE BEST WAY TO MOVE HEAVY GOODS.

THE COUNTRY GOODS WERE CARRIED BY WAGONS PULLED BY TEAMS OF HORSES.

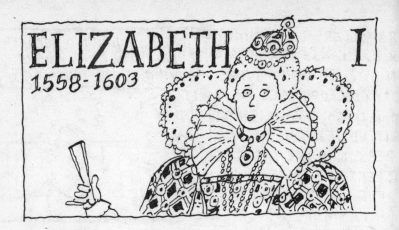

ELIZABETH I
1558-1603

When Elizabeth became queen she was faced with many problems. The treasury was empty. The crime-rate was high. Recent harvests had been bad. Catholics were worried about having a Protestant monarch again.

But Elizabeth was a tolerant woman of good sense and great ability. She brought peace and prosperity to the country and her reign was a long and glorious one (though there were many plots to assassinate her).

Elizabeth never married, but she had many suitors. Some were powerful men, like Philip of Spain (who had been married to her sister, Mary).

One of Elizabeth's faults was that she couldn't make decisions – she was always

OTHER COUNTRIES WERE NOT HAVING SUCH A PEACEFUL TIME. MANY OF THEIR CRAFTSMEN FLED TO ENGLAND. THEY WERE WELCOME BECAUSE THEY BROUGHT THEIR SKILLS. THE WEAVERS OF HOLLAND HELPED ENGLAND'S MOST IMPORTANT INDUSTRY - CLOTH-MAKING.

changing her mind. She certainly didn't make a decision about a husband. She kept all her suitors guessing. Maybe she did this on purpose. It was a clever way of confusing other kings and causing jealousy among them.

Besides, most of the other kings were Catholics and Elizabeth wanted England to stay a Protestant country.

DURING HER LIFETIME SHE RECEIVED 15 MARRIAGE PROPOSALS FROM ALL OVER EUROPE - SPAIN, FRANCE, SWEDEN, AUSTRIA, GERMANY, DENMARK, SCOTLAND, AS WELL AS ENGLAND.

PROPOSALS SO FAR
2 Kings
2 Princes
7 Dukes
2 Earls
1 Lord
1 Knight

Umm...

ELIZABETH & MARY QUEEN of SCOTS

Some of England's enemies were getting too close for comfort. Philip of Spain had sent troops to Ireland to help the Irish fight against the English.

Mary Queen of Scots had married the French king and Scotland was about to become part of France. Some Scottish nobles asked Elizabeth for help in pushing out French soldiers who were garrisoned in Scotland.

Elizabeth didn't approve of subjects rising up against their queen, but she secretly sent a fleet of ships to blockade the port of Leith near Edinburgh. The blockade was successful and the French surrendered.

ELIZABETH MAY HAVE BEEN JEALOUS OF MARY BECAUSE OF HER BEAUTY AND BECAUSE SHE HAD MARRIED AND HAD A CHILD. HENRY VII HAD BEEN THE GRANDFATHER OF BOTH MARY AND ELIZABETH SO MARY WAS NEXT IN LINE TO THE ENGLISH THRONE – UNLESS ELIZABETH HAD A CHILD.

When the King of France died, Mary Queen of Scots returned to Scotland. She soon found herself fighting with her nobles because they were Protestant and she was Catholic.

She fled into England and asked Elizabeth for protection. This was a tricky situation for Elizabeth. Mary had many supporters in England and abroad who thought she would make a better queen of England than Elizabeth.

Elizabeth kept Mary under house arrest in a castle for many years. She could not bring herself to make a decision about Mary's future. Eventually, she grew worried that Mary was plotting against her and had her executed.

DURING THIS TIME, MANY PEOPLE WERE KILLED BY DISEASES LIKE SMALLPOX, MEASLES AND THE PLAGUE. DOCTORS WERE NOT VERY KNOWLEDGEABLE AND KNEW HARDLY ANYTHING ABOUT THE HUMAN BODY. THEY TRIED TO CURE THEIR PATIENTS BY CHANGING THEIR DIET OR BLOOD-LETTING. THEY THOUGHT THAT AS BLOOD FLOWED OUT OF THE BODY, THE DISEASE WENT TOO. BARBERS NOT ONLY CUT HAIR, THEY LET BLOOD! THE RED AND WHITE POLES ABOVE THEIR SHOPS REPRESENTED BLOOD AND BANDAGES!

SAILORS and EXPLORERS THE BEGINNING OF AN EMPIRE

DURING HENRY VII'S REIGN, COLUMBUS DISCOVERED
THE AMERICAS. THIS INSPIRED ENGLISH SAILORS
TO SET OUT ON THEIR OWN VOYAGES OF DISCOVERY.
SOON, INTREPID SEAMEN WERE SAILING TO EVERY
CORNER OF THE GLOBE, RAIDING AND TRADING. THEY
ESPECIALLY LIKED ATTACKING THE SPANISH TREASURE

NORTH AMERICA

JOHN CABOT and MARTIN FROBISHER TRIED TO GET TO CHINA THIS WAY

EUROPE

ENGLISH SETTLEMENTS HERE

FRANCIS DRAKE WAS THE FIRST ENGLISHMAN TO SAIL ROUND THE WORLD

TREASURE SHIPS TO SPAIN

AFRICA

PACIFIC OCEAN

THE SPANISH MAIN

DRAKE SETS OFF ACROSS PACIFIC

SOUTH AMERICA

ATLANTIC OCEAN

DRAKE PLUNDERS SPANISH SETTLEMENTS

HIPS RETURNING FROM SOUTH AMERICA.
RADING POSTS WERE SET UP IN INDIA, ON THE
SLANDS OF THE FAR EAST AND ON THE COAST OF
NORTH AMERICA. THESE WOULD SOON BECOME
OLONIES OF THE BRITISH EMPIRE.
HE SLAVE TRADE STARTED WHEN SHIPS BEGAN TO TAKE
EOPLE FROM AFRICA TO THE WEST INDIES.

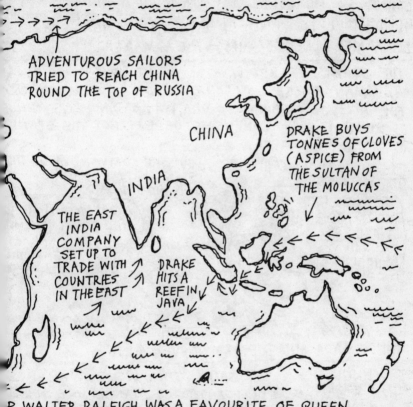

ADVENTUROUS SAILORS
TRIED TO REACH CHINA
ROUND THE TOP OF RUSSIA

CHINA

DRAKE BUYS
TONNES OF CLOVES
(A SPICE) FROM
THE SULTAN OF
THE MOLUCCAS

INDIA

THE EAST
INDIA
COMPANY
SET UP TO
TRADE WITH
COUNTRIES
IN THE EAST

DRAKE
HITS A
REEF IN
JAVA

R WALTER RALEIGH WAS A FAVOURITE OF QUEEN
IZABETH'S AT COURT. HE SAILED ON MANY ADVENTURES,
IDING SPANISH PORTS AND SHIPS IN SOUTH AMERICA.
BROUGHT HOME NEW THINGS— THE POTATO AND TOBACCO.
STARTED THE SETTLEMENT OF VIRGINIA IN NORTH AMERICA.

ARMADA!

RIGHT, I've had enough!!

KING PHILIP OF SPAIN GREW ANNOYED AT THE WAY THE ENGLISH WERE ATTACKING HIS SHIPS. BESIDES, HE THOUGHT ENGLAND WAS A GODLESS COUNTRY.

HE DECIDED TO CONQUER ENGLAND SO HE PREPARED AN ARMED FLEET OF SHIPS — THE ARMADA.

THE SPANISH FLEET WAS MADE UP OF 130 SHIPS WITH MANY LARGE GALLEONS. IT WAS COMMANDED BY THE DUKE OF MEDINA-SIDONIA, WHO HAD NO EXPERIENCE OF SHIPS AT ALL. CONFUSING ORDERS GOT THE SPANISH OFF TO A BAD START.

THE DUKE THOUGHT HIS ORDERS WERE...

> To meet up with the Spanish army when they land in England.

...BUT THE COMMANDER OF THE SPANISH ARMY BASED IN HOLLAND HAD SAID...

> Meet us in Holland and escort us across the Channel to England

THE ARMADA AND THE ARMY NEVER MET.

THE ENGLISH HAD 197 SHIPS. THEY WERE SMALLER THAN THE SPANISH ONES AND COULD MANOEUVRE QUICKLY. THEIR GUNS HAD A LONGER RANGE THAN THOSE OF THE SPANISH.

THE ENGLISH FLEET WAS COMMANDED BY LORD HOWARD OF EFFINGHAM WITH DRAKE AS HIS VICE-COMMANDER.

THE TWO FLEETS MET IN THE ENGLISH CHANNEL OFF
PLYMOUTH. THEY FOUGHT ON AND OFF FOR FIVE DAYS AS
THEY DRIFTED UP THE CHANNEL.

THE SPANISH RETREATED AND ANCHORED OFF THE
FRENCH PORT OF CALAIS. THE ENGLISH SENT IN
FIRESHIPS. MANY SPANISH SAILORS ABANDONED SHIP IN
TERROR. THE FLEET SET SAIL IN DISORDER.

A STORM BLEW UP AS THE SPANISH FLEET FLED
NORTHWARDS. THE SHIPS SAILED ROUND THE NORTH OF
SCOTLAND AND MANY
WERE WRECKED
OFF THE COAST
OF IRELAND.

FASHION

AT THE
BEGINNING
OF THE
STUART AGE
MEN WORE
THEIR HAIR
LONG. BEARDS
WERE STILL
IN FASHION.
MEN AND
WOMEN
WORE BROAD-
BRIMMED
HATS AND
AS MUCH
LACE AS
POSSIBLE.

→ JACK BOOTS

THE PURITANS
WORE DARK,
SIMPLE
CLOTHES BECAUSE
THEY THOUGHT
IT WAS SINFUL
TO DRESS
IN BRIGHT
COLOURS.

WIDE COLLARS
PROTECTED
CLOTHES
FROM LONG
HAIR.

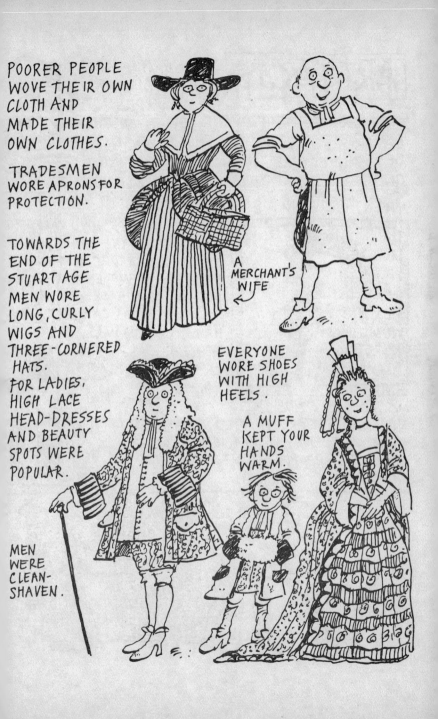

POORER PEOPLE WOVE THEIR OWN CLOTH AND MADE THEIR OWN CLOTHES.

TRADESMEN WORE APRONS FOR PROTECTION.

TOWARDS THE END OF THE STUART AGE MEN WORE LONG, CURLY WIGS AND THREE-CORNERED HATS.
FOR LADIES, HIGH LACE HEAD-DRESSES AND BEAUTY SPOTS WERE POPULAR.

MEN WERE CLEAN-SHAVEN.

A MERCHANT'S WIFE

EVERYONE WORE SHOES WITH HIGH HEELS.

A MUFF KEPT YOUR HANDS WARM.

ART FACTS

DURING THE REIGN OF THE TUDORS, ALL SORTS OF NEW IDEAS SUDDENLY ARRIVED FROM EUROPE. THIS EVENT WAS GIVEN THE NAME OF RENAISSANCE (REBIRTH). THERE WERE NEW STYLES OF ARCHITECTURE, MUSIC AND PAINTING. PEOPLE BEGAN TO TAKE AN INTEREST IN SCIENCE, NEW INVENTIONS AND MACHINERY.

A MERCHANT BY HOLBEIN

LARGE HOUSES HAD TAPESTRIE HANGING ON THE ROOM WALLS. THESE WERE DECORATIVE PICTURES OF WOVEN MATERIAL. BUT THE NEW FASHION FOR PAINTINGS WAS CATCHING ON. HANS HOLBEIN WAS A GERMAN PAINTER WHO PAINTED MANY OF THE PEOPLE AT HENRY VIII'S COURT.

NICHOLAS HILLIARD PAINTED MINIATURES. THESE WERE TINY PORTRAITS THAT COULD BE SENT TO PEOPLE, AS WE WOULD SEND PHOTOGRAPHS TODAY.

EVERYONE LIKED A GOOD SONG AND DANCE!

LUTE   VIOL   VIRGINALS

GOING TO THE THEATRE TO WATCH A PLAY
BECAME A VERY POPULAR ACTIVITY. LONDON HAD
MANY THEATRES. THEY WERE BUILT OUTSIDE THE CITY
WALLS BECAUSE CITY OFFICIALS DIDN'T APPROVE OF PLAYS.
WILLIAM SHAKESPEARE BECAME THE MOST IMPORTANT
PLAYWRIGHT OF THE
TIME. ALL SORTS OF
PEOPLE, RICH AND
POOR, WENT TO
THE THEATRE
ON A FINE
AFTERNOON.

PIPE AND TABOR

RECORDER

BAGPIPES

TRUMPET

THE STUARTS

When Elizabeth died childless, next in line to the throne was James VI of Scotland. He was the son of Elizabeth's one-time enemy, Mary Queen of Scots. James became the first Stuart king of England.

Scotland and England now shared the same monarch, but they remained separate countries for another hundred years.

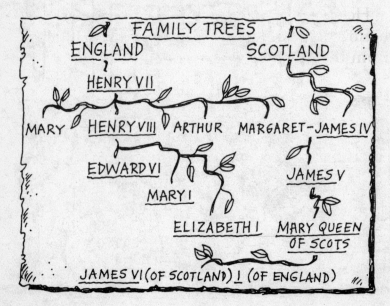

FAMILY TREES

ENGLAND   SCOTLAND

HENRY VII

MARY   HENRY VIII   ARTHUR   MARGARET — JAMES IV

EDWARD VI   JAMES V

MARY I

ELIZABETH I   MARY QUEEN OF SCOTS

JAMES VI (OF SCOTLAND) I (OF ENGLAND)

In James's time, the king and his advisors still ran the country from the royal court. Parliament met only occasionally, as in Tudor times.

However, throughout the Stuart age, the business of running the country slowly shifted from the monarch to Parliament.

England continued to be a Protestant country, but now people began to choose their own religion. There were still many who disliked the idea of a Protestant ruler. The monarch was never safe from the danger of assassination. James VI wore specially padded clothes because of his terror of being stabbed.

In the Stuart age, England became a wealthy and more powerful nation.

Most people still lived and worked in the country. Many made their living from the sea as fishermen or traders.

English trading ships sailed all round Europe, to America and the Far East. They carried coal, iron and timber. Wool and cloth were the main exports.

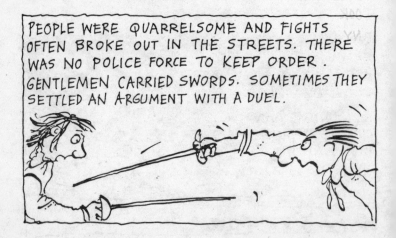

PEOPLE WERE QUARRELSOME AND FIGHTS OFTEN BROKE OUT IN THE STREETS. THERE WAS NO POLICE FORCE TO KEEP ORDER. GENTLEMEN CARRIED SWORDS. SOMETIMES THEY SETTLED AN ARGUMENT WITH A DUEL.

PEOPLE WERE STILL PUBLICLY PUNISHED AND EXECUTED. FOR MINOR CRIMES YOU COULD BE PUT IN THE STOCKS OR THE PILLORY.

FOR GREATER CRIMES NOBLES WERE BEHEADED AND ORDINARY FOLK WERE HANGED. THE BODIES OF THIEVES WERE LEFT HANGING ON THE GIBBET. THE HEADS OF TRAITORS WERE PLACED ON SPIKES FOR ALL TO SEE.

EVERYONE BELIEVED IN MAGIC AND WITCHCRAFT. KING JAMES I WROTE A BOOK ABOUT WITCHES.

ANY UNUSUAL BEHAVIOUR COULD BE SEEN AS A SIGN OF WITCHCRAFT.

MEN, WOMEN AND CHILDREN WERE BURNT AT THE STAKE AS WITCHES.

Evil magic potion, my foot! This is cabbage soup.

JAMES
1603-1625
VI AND I

As soon as Queen Elizabeth died, a messenger set out for Scotland with the news. The journey took him two and a half days. This was a record as royal messengers usually took five days to reach Edinburgh from London.

James set out immediately on his journey south.

SCOTLAND WAS A VERY POOR COUNTRY. JAMES WAS KEEN TO REACH THE RICH SOUTH BUT HE TRAVELLED SLOWLY, BEING FED AND ENTERTAINED ALL THE WAY BY WEALTHY FAMILIES KEEN TO GET ON THE RIGHT SIDE OF THE NEW KING!

We've already eaten but if you insist...

James was a kind yet greedy man. He was very well educated, but gave the impression of being a bit of a fool.

He was addicted to hunting and usually appeared at court spattered with mud because he had been out riding all day.

James believed that God had chosen him to be king and therefore people should always obey him. This led to arguments with members of Parliament and others who thought the king was getting above himself.

Two groups of people were unhappy that England was to remain officially a Protestant country. They were the Puritans and the Catholics. Some of them decided to take action . . .

THE PURITANS WANTED TO 'PURIFY' THE PROTESTANT RELIGION. THEY DRESSED VERY PLAINLY AND LED A SIMPLE LIFE. THEY WERE BECOMING MORE POWERFUL IN THE COUNTRY BUT SOME THOUGHT THEY COULD HAVE A BETTER LIFE ELSEWHERE. MANY OF THEM SET SAIL FOR AMERICA ABOARD THE 'MAYFLOWER'.

REMEMBER! REMEMBER! THE FIFTH of NOVEMBER

SOME CATHOLICS DECIDED TO TAKE MORE DRASTIC ACTION THAN THE PURITANS...

PLOT! SCHEME! PLOT!

THEIR FIRST IDEA WAS TO ABDUCT THE KING'S CHILDREN. THEN THEY DECIDED TO ASSASSINATE THE KING. WHEN HE CAME TO OPEN PARLIAMENT ON 5TH NOVEMBER 1605, THEY WOULD BLOW UP THE BUILDING. THEY RENTED A HOUSE NEARBY

AS THEIR HEADQUARTERS. 36 BARRELS OF GUNPOWDER WERE BROUGHT ACROSS THE RIVER UNDER COVER OF DARKNESS. THEY WERE HIDDEN IN THE CELLARS UNDER THE HOUSES OF PARLIAMENT.

ONE OF THE CONSPIRATORS BEGAN TO FEEL GUILTY ABOUT SENDING HUNDREDS OF PEOPLE TO THEIR DEATHS. HE WROTE AN ANONYMOUS LETTER TO A LORD...

JAMES COMMANDED THAT A NEW BIBLE BE PRODUCED. 47 SCHOLARS WORKED FOR 4 YEARS TO PRODUCE IT. IT IS KNOWN AS THE KING JAMES BIBLE OR THE AUTHORIZED VERSION AND IS STILL IN USE TODAY.

James was a peace-loving man and he wanted an end to wars with other countries. He made peace with Spain. There was no more fighting with Scotland since England and Scotland shared the same king.

James was a terrible spendthrift and he was always short of money. Parliament tried to control the king's expensive life-style, but to no avail.

Avoid Parliament! It will receive a terrible blow!

THE CELLARS WERE RAIDED AND GUY FAWKES WAS FOUND WAITING TO LIGHT THE FUSE. HE WAS ARRESTED AND TORTURED UNTIL HE GAVE THE NAMES OF HIS ACCOMPLICES. THEY WERE ALL EXECUTED.

TRAVEL

TRAVEL WAS BECOMING MUCH QUICKER BUT THERE WAS SO MUCH WHEELED TRAFFIC ON THE ROADS THAT THEY WERE IN VERY BAD CONDITION. IN WINTER, RUTS AND POTHOLES FILLED WITH WATER AND ROADS BECAME IMPASSABLE. TO REMEDY THIS TOLLS WERE INTRODUCED. AT SEVERAL POINTS ALONG THE MAIN ROUTES TRAVELLERS HAD TO PAY A FEE. THE MONEY WENT TO REPAIR THE ROADS.

A TOLL GATE

TOLL-KEEPER'S HOUSE

RICH PEOPLE WOULD TRAVEL IN THEIR OWN COACHES.

Follow that Sedan chair!

A SEDAN CHAIR COULD BE EASILY CARRIED THROUGH NARROW CITY LANES. IT SAVED WELL-DRESSED PEOPLE FROM GETTING THEIR CLOTHES MUDDY.

IN LONDON IT WAS OFTEN QUICKER TO TRAVEL BY BOAT ON THE THAMES.

COACHES AND WAGONS CARRIED MESSAGES AND PARCELS. THE ROYAL MAIL STARTED IN THE REIGN OF CHARLES I.

LETTERS WERE FOLDED AND CLOSED WITH SEALING-WAX.

STAGE COACHES BEGAN TO RUN BETWEEN LARGE TOWNS. LONG DISTANCES WERE TRAVELLED IN 'STAGES'. THE PASSENGERS WOULD STAY THE NIGHT AT VARIOUS INNS ALONG THE ROUTE. THE JOURNEY FROM LONDON TO YORK TOOK ABOUT A WEEK.

IN TOWN PEOPLE COULD HIRE A LINK-BOY TO LIGHT THE WAY HOME AFTER DARK.

AT SCHOOL and AT PLAY

ABCDEF
GHIJKL
MNOPQ
RSTUVW
XYZ abcd
efghijklm
nopqrstuv
wxyz

HORN BOOKS WERE WOODEN BATS COVERED WITH A THIN LAYER OF HORN FOR PROTECTION. THEY WERE USED TO TEACH CHILDREN THE ALPHABET.

MANY TOWNS AND VILLAGES NOW HAD SCHOOLS. IT WAS USUALLY ONLY THE SONS OF RICH FAMILIES OR WELL-TO-DO MERCHANTS WHO WENT TO THEM.

GIRLS WERE TAUGHT AT HOME. THEY LEARNED HOW TO COOK, SEW, PLAY A MUSICAL INSTRUMENT AND HOW TO BEHAVE IN PUBLIC. THE MAJORITY OF THE POPULATION NEVER LEARNED TO READ. MANY PEOPLE DIDN'T LEARN ARITHMETIC UNTIL THEY WERE ADULTS.

TOYS WERE MADE OF PAINTED WOOD.

THROUGHOUT THE YEAR THERE WERE PUBLIC
HOLIDAYS LIKE BARTHOLOMEW FAIR OR MIDSUMMER
EVE. PEOPLE COULD LET THEIR HAIR DOWN, ENJOY
THEMSELVES AND WATCH ACROBATS AND WRESTLERS.

COFFEE-DRINKING
BECAME VERY POPULAR
AND COFFEE HOUSES
SPRANG UP
EVERYWHERE.
THEY WERE MOSTLY
USED BY MEN. THEY
SOON BECAME
PLACES WHERE
BUSINESS WAS DONE.
WHILE DRINKING
COFFEE YOU
COULD READ A
NEWS SHEET OR
'BOOK'. THESE SOON
BECAME 'NEWSPAPERS'.

CHARLES I
1625-1649

Charles was a quiet and serious man. He had been a sickly child and was not very tall. He stammered when he spoke.

He was a lover of music and drama and owned a large collection of paintings.

CHARLES BROUGHT THE DUTCH PAINTER PAUL RUBENS FROM HOLLAND TO DECORATE THE CEILING OF HIS NEW BANQUETING HALL.
ANOTHER DUTCH ARTIST, ANTHONY VAN DYCK, BECAME COURT PAINTER AND PAINTED MANY BEAUTIFUL PORTRAITS.
HIS FAMOUS PAINTING OF THE KING IN THREE POSITIONS WAS PROBABLY MADE SO THE SCULPTOR BERNINI COULD CARVE A BUST.

Like his father, Charles believed that God had appointed him king. This made him rather arrogant and led to many arguments with Parliament.

The king dismissed Parliament and ruled without it for eleven years.

When Parliament was recalled, arguments soon broke out again. The king demanded that they give him more money.

Eventually, Charles walked into the Houses of Parliament with an armed guard. He wanted to arrest a group of MPs he thought were troublemakers. The king said:

I have come to arrest those guilty of treason!

BUT THE MEMBERS OF PARLIAMENT HAD FLED.

I see the birds have flown!

ALL THE MEMBERS OF PARLIAMENT FELT THEY HAD BEEN INSULTED. NO MONARCH HAD EVER TREATED PARLIAMENT LIKE THIS.
IT WAS CLEAR THAT FIGHTING WAS GOING TO BREAK OUT SOON. THE CIVIL WAR WAS ABOUT TO BEGIN BETWEEN THOSE WHO SUPPORTED THE KING AND THOSE WHO SUPPORTED PARLIAMENT.

THE CIVIL WAR

KING CHARLES WITHDREW NORTH.

HE RAISED HIS ROYAL STANDARD AT NOTTINGHAM AND APPEALED FOR SUPPORT.

THE STANDARD BLEW DOWN IN A GALE – A BAD OMEN!

PARLIAMENT GATHERED AN ARMY OF 13,000 MEN COMMANDED BY THE EARL OF ESSEX.

CHARLES COLLECTED AN ARMY AND MOVED SOUTH TO OXFORD WHERE HE SET UP HIS HEADQUARTERS.

THE NAVY JOINED PARLIAMENT'S SIDE AND CUT OFF ANY HELP THE KING MIGHT HAVE GOT FROM ABROAD.

A POODLE BELONGING TO PRINCE RUPERT (THE KING'S NEPHEW) BECAME A MASCOT FOR THE ROYALIST ARMY.

THE SCOTS JOINED THE SIDE OF PARLIAMENT. THE KING'S SUPPORTERS IN THE NORTH WERE CAUGHT BETWEEN TWO ARMIES.

NEWCASTLE

YORK

BATTLES AND SKIRMISHES RAGED UP AND DOWN THE COUNTRY. AFTER DEFEAT AT THE BATTLE OF MARSTON MOOR, PRINCE RUPERT HAD TO HIDE IN A BEAN FIELD.

BOTH SIDES
IN THE CIVIL
WAR HAD
DIFFICULTY IN
FINDING
EQUIPMENT
FOR THEIR
ARMIES.
SOMETIMES
OFFICERS MISTOOK
THEIR OWN MEN
FOR THE ENEMY,
SO ALIKE WERE
THEIR CLOTHES.

THE KING AND THE ROYALIST ARMY WERE SUPPORTED BY
THE CAVALIERS, WHO WERE USUALLY MEMBERS OF NOBLE
FAMILIES.

SOME OF THE
TROOPS ON
PARLIAMENT'S
SIDE WERE
CALLED
ROUNDHEADS
(BECAUSE OF
THEIR SHORT
HAIR) OR
LOBSTERS
(BECAUSE THE
BACKS OF
THEIR HELMETS
LOOKED LIKE
LOBSTERS'
TAILS).

SOME OF THE
LEADERS OF
PARLIAMENT'S
TROOPS WANTED
MORE EFFICIENCY.
WHEN MEN WERE
CALLED TO FIGHT,
TRADE AND INDUSTRY
IN THE TOWNS
AND COUNTRYSIDE
CAME TO A
STANDSTILL.
WHAT WAS
NEEDED
WAS A FULL-TIME

PIKEMAN
AND
GUNNER

PROFESSIONAL ARMY. SO AN ARMY – CALLED THE NEW
MODEL ARMY– WAS CREATED. ONE OF THE LEADERS OF
THE NEW ARMY WAS OLIVER CROMWELL, A COUNTRY
GENTLEMAN. HE WAS SOON TO BECOME A VERY POWERFUL
MAN.

THE END OF THE CIVIL WAR
CAME WHEN THE KING AND
PRINCE RUPERT WERE
DEFEATED AT THE BATTLE
OF NASEBY.

CHARLES HANDED HIMSELF
OVER TO THE SCOTS. THE
SCOTS EVENTUALLY GAVE HIM
TO THE ENGLISH.

BY NOW, THE ARMY, UNDER OLIVER CROMWELL, HAD MORE POWER THAN PARLIAMENT. THEY WANTED CHARLES OUT OF THE WAY.

CHARLES WAS BROUGHT TO TRIAL AND SENTENCED.

Tyrant, traitor and public enemy to the good people of this nation!

CHARLES WAS BEHEADED OUTSIDE THE BANQUETING HALL IN WHITEHALL.

OLIVER CROMWELL WAS NOW IN CHARGE OF THE COUNTRY.

CROMWELL GAVE HIMSELF THE TITLE OF LORD PROTECTOR. ENGLAND, WALES, SCOTLAND AND IRELAND WERE NOW UNDER MILITARY RULE. CROMWELL AND HIS MEN WERE UNPOPULAR. THEY WERE PURITANS AND WANTED PEOPLE TO LIVE AN HONEST (BUT DULL) LIFE. THEATRES WERE CLOSED AND MUSIC, DANCING AND SINGING WERE FROWNED UPON.
AFTER ONLY A FEW YEARS IN POWER, CROMWELL DIED. HIS SON RICHARD BECAME THE NEW PROTECTOR.

RICHARD CROMWELL WAS NOT AS CLEVER AS HIS FATHER. HE WAS UNPOPULAR AND HE FLED TO FRANCE. CHARLES I's SON WAS PROCLAIMED KING.

FOODY SUBJECTS

FOOD WAS STILL COOKED OVER AN OPEN FIRE OR BAKED IN A BRICK OVEN.

THERE WERE NOW COOKERY BOOKS FILLED WITH RECIPES.

ALL SORTS OF DELICACIES AND NEW RECIPES WERE ARRIVING FROM ABROAD. FRENCH FOOD WAS ALL THE RAGE AND THINGS LIKE MACARONI AND SAGO WERE POPULAR. SOME FOREIGNERS HAD A DIM VIEW OF ENGLISH COOKING...

The meat is always under-done, served up under a rampart of five or six heaps of cabbage, carrots, turnips, well peppered and swimming in butter!

NEW DRINKS FROM ABROAD

TEA FROM CHINA

COFFEE FROM ARABIA

CHOCOLATE FROM THE WEST INDIES

BREAKFAST WAS EATEN JUST AFTER GETTING UP. IT WOULD BE BREAD AND BUTTER, COLD MEAT, ALE, TEA OR COFFEE.

RICH FAMILIES NO LONGER ATE IN A GREAT HALL WITH THEIR GUESTS AND SERVANTS. THEY NOW HAD DINING-ROOMS WHERE MEALS WERE MORE PRIVATE.

DINNER WAS EATEN AT MIDDAY AND WAS THE MAIN MEAL. THERE WOULD BE ROAST MEATS, VEGETABLES AND SWEET PUDDINGS – BUT ALL SERVED AT THE SAME TIME AND PEOPLE COULD EAT THEM HOW THEY CHOSE. THERE WOULD BE FRUIT AND CHEESE TO FINISH.

TABLES HAD TABLECLOTHS OVER THEM. DISHES WERE MADE OF PEWTER OR BRIGHTLY COLOURED POTTERY. POOR FOLK STILL USED WOODEN PLATES AND BOWLS.

FORKS WERE NOW IN USE BUT CUTLERY WAS A DIFFERENT SHAPE FROM TODAY'S.

SUPPER WAS EATEN IN THE EARLY EVENING. THE FOOD WAS SIMILAR TO DINNER BUT ONLY ONE OR TWO DISHES. AFTERWARDS, PEOPLE LIKED TO TALK, AND PLAY MUSIC OR SING.

CHARLES II
1660-1685

After the Civil War, when Cromwell was still Protector, it was forbidden to proclaim anyone king in England. However, Charles II was proclaimed king in Ulster and Scotland. He travelled to Scotland from France, where he had been staying. When Cromwell heard that Charles had been crowned king in Scotland, he marched north with an army.

Charles went south with some troops but he was soon a fugitive. He hid in trees and ditches until he could catch a boat to France.

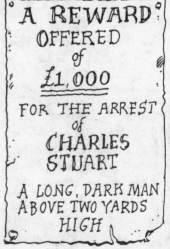

A REWARD OFFERED of £1,000 FOR THE ARREST of CHARLES STUART A LONG, DARK MAN ABOVE TWO YARDS HIGH

Charles had to wait until Cromwell died before he was invited back to England as king. The event became known as the Restoration.

He was a cheerful, easy-going man who liked to enjoy himself. He was content to let others run the country as official meetings bored him.

He was a keen sportsman and played tennis every day. He also liked to watch horse-racing and raced his own yacht on the Thames.

SCIENCE

UP UNTIL THIS TIME SCIENCE HAD BEEN A RATHER DODGY BUSINESS. ALCHEMISTS SPENT THEIR TIME DOING STRANGE EXPERIMENTS – LIKE TRYING TO TURN ORDINARY METALS INTO GOLD. THEY MIXED POTIONS OF HERBS AND POWDERS – ALONG WITH A DASH OF MAGIC!

I was this day admitted to the Royal Society on signing a book and being taken by the hand by the President. But it is a most acceptable thing to hear their discourses and see their experiments,

Curse my coat! You're supposed to be a diamond!

IN THE STUART AGE SCIENTISTS BEGAN TO LOOK AT THE REAL FACTS.

CHARLES II WAS INTERESTED IN SCIENCE. HE FOUNDED THE ROYAL SOCIETY, WHICH HELD REGULAR MEETINGS WHERE SCIENTISTS COULD EXCHANGE INFORMATION AND CARRY OUT EXPERIMENTS. NOT ALL THE MEMBERS WERE SCIENTISTS. THE FAMOUS DIARY-WRITER, SAMUEL PEPYS, JOINED AND NOTED THE EVENT IN HIS DIARY...

which was this day on the nature of fire and how it goes out in a place where the ayre is not free and sooner out when the ayre is exhausted.

TWO OF THE FIRST MEMBERS OF THE ROYAL
SOCIETY WERE ISAAC NEWTON AND EDMUND HALLEY.

NEWTON WAS A PROFESSOR
OF MATHEMATICS. HE MADE
A STUDY OF LIGHT AND HOW
IT COULD BE SPLIT INTO
COLOURS (LIKE A RAINBOW)
WHICH HE CALLED A
SPECTRUM.
AFTER HE SAW AN APPLE
DROP FROM A TREE HE
BEGAN HIS STUDY OF GRAVITY
AND THE MOVEMENT OF THE
PLANETS.

CHARLES II ALSO
FOUNDED THE ROYAL
OBSERVATORY AT
GREENWICH. THIS WAS
FOR THE STUDY OF THE
STARS WHICH WOULD
HELP SHIPS TO
NAVIGATE.

THE ASTRONOMER-
ROYAL, EDMUND HALLEY,
MADE A STUDY OF
THE COMET WHICH WAS
NAMED AFTER HIM.

DISEASE and DISASTER

Two disasters struck London during Charles's reign.

The fatal disease called the Plague had been around for centuries. The Great Plague of 1665 seemed particularly bad. A third of the city's population died.

The Plague was spread by the fleas of the black rats which roamed the filthy streets of London. No one knew this at the time, so the disease seemed mysterious and horrifying.

THE GREAT FIRE of LONDON 1666

THE FIRE STARTED IN PUDDING LANE. THE KING'S BAKER, THOMAS FARRINOR, LEFT A PILE OF WOOD TOO NEAR HIS OVEN...

...AN INN-YARD FILLED WITH HAY WAS THE NEXT TO GO...

...THEN A ROW OF WAREHOUSES FILLED WITH TALLOW, OIL AND SPIRITS.

BLAM!

THE STREETS OF LONDON WERE SO NARROW THAT THE FLAMES COULD EASILY LEAP FROM ONE HOUSE TO THE NEXT. MOST OF THE BUILDINGS WERE MADE OF WOOD AND BURNT QUICKLY.

SAILORS WERE BROUGHT FROM THE RIVER TO BLOW UP BUILDINGS IN THE FIRE'S PATH AND TRY TO STOP THE FIRE SPREADING.
A STRONG WIND HELPED TO FAN THE FLAMES. WHEN IT WAS ALL OVER 100,000 HOMELESS WERE CAMPING IN THE SURROUNDING FIELDS. OVER 80 CHURCHES HAD BEEN DESTROYED, ALONG WITH ST PAUL'S CATHEDRAL.

BUILDINGS

AFTER THE GREAT FIRE, THE ARCHITECT CHRISTOPHER WREN DREW UP PLANS FOR A MAGNIFICENT NEW LONDON. THERE WOULD BE WIDE STREETS, FINE BUILDINGS AND VIEWS.

HOWEVER, PEOPLE WERE IMPATIENT TO REBUILD THEIR HOUSES AND WORKSHOPS. WREN'S PLAN WAS NEVER USED, THOUGH HE DESIGNED THE NEW ST PAUL'S CATHEDRAL AND MANY OF THE CITY'S CHURCHES.

INIGO JONES FIRST MADE HIS NAME AS A DESIGNER OF MASQUES. THESE WERE A CROSS BETWEEN A PARTY AND A PERFORMANCE WITH DANCE, MUSIC, SONGS AND ELABORATE COSTUMES. HE THEN TURNED TO ARCHITECTURE AFTER A TRIP TO ITALY WHERE HE PICKED UP NEW IDEAS. HIS MOST FAMOUS BUILDING IS THE BANQUETING HALL, WHITEHALL, LONDON.

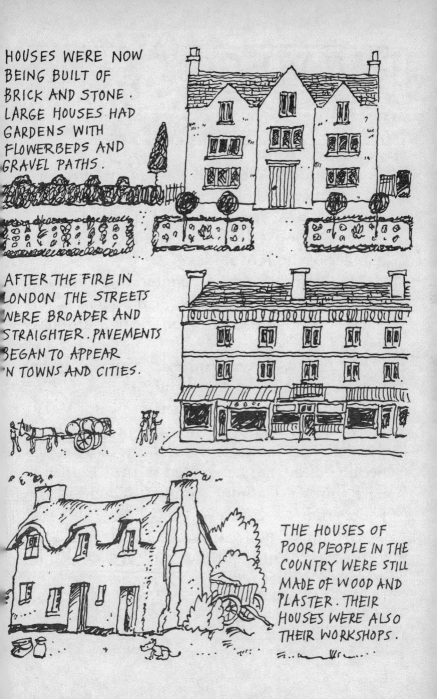

HOUSES WERE NOW
BEING BUILT OF
BRICK AND STONE.
LARGE HOUSES HAD
GARDENS WITH
FLOWERBEDS AND
GRAVEL PATHS.

AFTER THE FIRE IN
LONDON THE STREETS
WERE BROADER AND
STRAIGHTER. PAVEMENTS
BEGAN TO APPEAR
IN TOWNS AND CITIES.

THE HOUSES OF
POOR PEOPLE IN THE
COUNTRY WERE STILL
MADE OF WOOD AND
PLASTER. THEIR
HOUSES WERE ALSO
THEIR WORKSHOPS.

Charles II died childless, so his brother James became king. James was a military man. He had been a general in the French army. During Charles's reign he was commander of the Royal Navy.

As a king, he took more interest in running the country than his brother had done.

He was not a pleasant man, being humourless and stubborn.

His first wife was Anne Hyde, who gave him two daughters, Mary and Anne.

He then married an Italian princess, Mary of Modena. Mary was a Catholic, so James decided to become a Catholic too. It soon became clear that he wanted to turn England back into a Catholic country again. Most people didn't want this.

The Duke of Monmouth led a rebellion against the king but he was defeated and executed. Other rebels were dealt with by the cruel Judge Jeffreys.

HANG EM!

Then Mary of Modena gave birth to a son. This was the last straw. The people were unhappy with a Catholic king, so they didn't want a Catholic heir to the throne as well.

The people turned to James's daughter Mary, who had married William of Orange, in Holland. (He was also James's nephew.) Both were Protestants and they were invited to become king and queen of England.

William landed with an army on the south coast of England. However, it was a peaceful invasion and became known as the Glorious Revolution. James helped matters by fleeing to France.

JAMES TRIED TWICE TO ESCAPE THE COUNTRY. THE FIRST TIME HE WAS CAUGHT BY SOME FISHERMEN. THE SECOND TIME HE WAS LUCKY.

Who 'ave we got 'ere then?

FASHION

MEN WORE SHIRTS OF LINEN OR SILK UNDER A DOUBLET OR JERKIN. EVERYONE WORE HOSE, WHICH WERE LIKE TIGHTS. WEALTHY MEN WORE PADDED CLOTHES WHICH WERE SLIT TO SHOW THE LINING.

LABOURERS WORE BOOTS OR LEGGINGS

NEARLY EVERYONE WORE A HAT - EVEN INDOORS

EARLY TUDOR STYLE

LATE TUDOR STYLE

RUFF

MEN WHO WORKED INDOORS - MERCHANTS, JUDGES, BANKERS ETC. - WORE LONG GOWNS. THEY WERE OFTEN TRIMMED WITH FUR.

EARRINGS AND NEAT BEARDS WERE POPULAR. SHOES HAD NO HEELS. BOOTS WORN FOR HUNTING.

RICH PEOPLE WORE BRIGHTLY COLOURED CLOTHES.
POORER PEOPLE WERE ONLY ALLOWED TO WEAR CERTAIN
COLOURS AND MATERIALS. THEY COULD BE PUNISHED IF
THEY DISOBEYED THESE RULES.

YOUNG WOMEN
WORE THEIR
HAIR
LONG.
MARRIED
WOMEN
KEPT
THEIR
HAIR
COVERED.

GABLE
HOOD →

EARLY
TUDOR
STYLE

LARGE
RUFF →

LATE →
TUDOR
STYLE

DRESSES WERE WORN OVER A
WIRE OR WHALEBONE FRAME
CALLED A FARTHINGALE. THIS
MADE THEM STICK OUT.

CHILDREN WORE
EXACTLY THE
SAME TYPES
OF CLOTHES
AS ADULTS.

WILLIAM & MARY

III
1689-1702

II
1689-1694

When Mary heard she was to be married to the dull William of Orange, she cried for a day and a half. However, the marriage turned out to be a happy one.

The couple were both interested in architecture and gardening. They asked Christopher Wren to redesign Hampton Court Palace. He also built them a new palace at Kensington.

King James made an attempt at getting his kingdom back. He landed in Ireland and raised an army, but was defeated by William at the Battle of the Boyne.

JAMES BESIEGED THE CITY OF LONDONDERRY FOR 105 DAYS. THOUSANDS DIED OF STARVATION AND DISEASE. THE SIEGE ENDED WHEN RELIEF CAME BY SEA.

James had supporters in Scotland too. Viscount Dundee started a rebellion, but his army was defeated at the Battle of Killiecrankie.

THE SCOTTISH REBELS WERE GIVEN A CERTAIN AMOUNT OF TIME IN WHICH TO SWEAR ALLEGIANCE TO KING WILLIAM. THE MACDONALD CLAN FAILED TO MAKE THE DEADLINE. SOLDIERS WERE SENT TO DEAL WITH THEM. SOME OF THE CLAN MANAGED TO ESCAPE INTO THE SNOW-COVERED MOUNTAINS. MOST WERE KILLED IN WHAT BECAME KNOWN AS THE MASSACRE OF GLEN COE.

In Parliament the MPs were beginning to divide themselves into political parties for the first time. Parliament met more often and had more power to run the country than in the past.

Mary died eight years before her husband. William met his end when he fell from his horse as it stumbled on a molehill.

OUTSIDE and IN

WALKING IN THE OPEN
AIR BECAME A POPULAR
PASTIME. LONDON HAD
MANY SQUARES AND PARKS
WHERE YOU COULD RIDE
OR STROLL OR PLAY A
SPORT LIKE GOLF OR
PELL-MELL.
CRICKET STARTED AT
THIS TIME AND THERE
WERE ROWDY GAMES
OF FOOTBALL.

GARDENS WERE PLANTED WITH ROWS OF TREES AND
BROAD PATHS CRISS-CROSSED BETWEEN FORMAL
FLOWERBEDS.

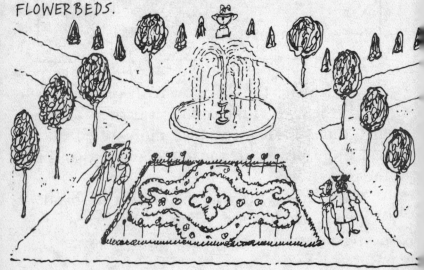

FURNITURE WAS MORE ELEGANT AND MORE COMFORTABLE THAN IN TUDOR TIMES.

COAL REPLACED LOGS IN THE FIRE.

CHAIRS AND SOFAS HAD PADDED SEATS AND BACKS. TABLES AND CHAIRS HAD CURVING LEGS. PAINTINGS WERE HUNG ON THE WALLS AND BOOKCASES AND CHESTS OF DRAWERS MADE AN APPEARANCE. FLOORS WERE USUALLY VARNISHED BOARDS.

WALLS WERE OFTEN COVERED IN WOODEN PANELS. CEILINGS WERE DECORATED WITH ORNATE PLASTER.

ROOMS WERE LIT BY CANDLES. THESE WERE VERY EXPENSIVE. POOR PEOPLE USUALLY MADE DO WITH THE LIGHT OF THE FIRE OR WENT TO BED AT DUSK.

ANNE
1702-1714

As Mary and William had no children, it was Mary's sister Anne who became the next queen.

Anne was dumpy, dull and always in poor health. However, she was dignified and tried hard to please and be a good monarch.

On the one hand, Anne's reign was seen as a glorious time for England. The country had become very wealthy. More and more land was being added to her empire round the world.

On the other hand, there were still many poor people in the countryside. People talked fearfully about 'The Mob', meaning gangs of ruffians who often marched violently through city streets.

For most of Anne's reign, England was at war with France. The Duke of Marlborough fought many successful campaigns against the French. His grateful nation built Blenheim Palace for him (named after one of his victorious battles). However, Anne fell out with the Duke and his wife, who was her best friend.

The Scots and the English were no longer on good terms. The English were afraid that Scotland might become an ally of one of England's enemies, like France.

To stop this happening, it was decided that the two parliaments should merge. Scotland and England became the United Kingdom.

SHE HAD SUFFERED SO MUCH ILLNESS DURING HER LIFE THAT WHEN SHE DIED HER DOCTOR SAID...

I believe death was as welcome to her as sleep is to a weary traveller.

ART FACTS

THEATRES HAD BEEN CLOSED BY THE PURITANS
DURING OLIVER CROMWELL'S TIME. THEY RE-OPENED
AFTER THE RESTORATION AND BECAME MORE POPULAR
THAN EVER.

IN TUDOR TIMES, THEATRES WERE OPEN TO THE
SKY. NOW THEY HAD ROOFS AND THE STAGE WAS LIT
BY CANDLES. THERE WAS PAINTED SCENERY AND ALL
SORTS OF SPECTACULAR SPECIAL EFFECTS WORKED BY
MACHINERY. WOMEN WERE ALLOWED TO ACT ON STAGE
FOR THE FIRST TIME.

OPERAS WERE NOW
BEING PERFORMED IN
THEATRES. PEOPLE
COULD BUY THE WORDS
AND MUSIC OF THEIR
FAVOURITE SONGS
AND SING THEM AT
HOME.

SINGING, DANCING
AND PLAYING MUSIC
WERE POPULAR HOME
ENTERTAINMENTS FOR
EVERYONE.

A collection of the
Newest and Best
SONGS and DANCES
~ from ~
THE INDIAN QUEEN

Most of the songs being
within the compass of
the FLUTE with bass
accompaniment for
HARPSICHORD or ORGAN

price one shilling

Act of Union 24
Anne 82, 90–91
Anne of Cleves 21
Armada, Spanish (1588) 48–9
armour 28, 29
art, Stuart 92–3
art, Tudor 52–3

Battles
    Bosworth (1485) 14
    the Boyne (1690) 86
    Flodden (1513) 25
    Killiecrankie (1689) 87
    Marston Moor 68
    Naseby (1645) 70
bear-baiting 17
Beefeaters 29
Bible 33, 61
bishops 22
Blenheim Palace 91
blood-letting 45
Boleyn, Anne 20
British Empire 47
buildings, Stuart 80–81
buildings, Tudor 30–31
burning at the stake 39, 57

Cabot, John 46
Calais 39, 49
castles 30
Catherine of Aragon 20
Catholics 9, 38–9, 42, 43, 45, 59,
    60, 82, 83
Cavaliers 69

Central America 37
Charles I 63, 66–8
Charles II 74–8, 82
China 46, 47
Church of England 21
cities 30, 31, 63, 81, 90
Civil War, the 67–71
cloth 24, 43, 56
clothes, Tudor 50–51
Columbus, Christopher 37, 46
cooking 36, 72
courtiers 8, 10
craftsmen 43
Cromwell, Oliver 70–71, 74, 75,
    92
Cromwell, Richard 71
Cromwell, Thomas 19

disease 45, 78
Drake, Sir Francis 46, 47, 48
drinks 37, 72
duels 56
Dundee Rebellion 87

East India Company 47
Edward IV 15
Edward VI 20, 32–3
Elizabeth I 13, 17, 20, 42–5, 47,
    54, 58
English Channel 48, 49
explorers 48–9

fashion, Stuart 84–5
fashion, Tudor 50–51

Fawkes, Guy 61
Field of Cloth-of-Gold 25
food, Stuart 72–3
food, Tudor 36–7
France 25, 39, 44, 91
Frobisher, Martin 46
furniture 34–5, 89

Glencoe, Massacre of (1692) 87
Glorious Revolution 83
Great Fire of London 78–9, 80, 81
Great Harry (a ship) 26–7
Great Plague (1665) 78
Grey, Lady Jane 33
Gunpowder Plot (1605) 60–61
guns 29

Halley, Edmund 77
Hampton Court Palace 86
Henry VII 9, 14–15, 44, 46
Henry VIII 18–26, 32, 33, 52
highwaymen 40, 41
houses 30–31, 80, 81
Howard, Catherine 21
Howard of Effingham, Lord 48
Hyde, Anne 82

inns 17, 35, 41, 63
Ireland 44, 49, 86

James II 82–3, 86
James VI of Scotland and I of England 54–9, 61
Jeffreys, Judge 82
Jones, Inigo 80

kings and queens
    Tudor 8, 9, 10, 11, 13, 17

landowners 24
Latin 9, 33
Leith 44

London 63, 78–81, 88
Londonderry 86

magic 57, 76
Marlborough, Duke of 91
Mary I 20, 32, 33, 38–9, 42
Mary II 82, 83
Mary of Modena 82, 83
Mary Queen of Scots 44–5, 54
Mayflower 59
Medina-Sidonia, Duke of 48
mercenaries 28
merchants 30, 64
Milford Haven 14
monarchs, see kings and queens
monasteries 22–3
Monmouth Rebellion 82
music, Stuart 71, 73, 80, 93
music, Tudor 52–3

New Model Army 70–71
newspapers 65
Newton, Sir Isaac 77
Northumberland, Duke of 32–3

painters
    Anthony Van Dyck 66
    Hans Holbein 52
    Nicholas Hilliard 52
    Paul Rubens 66
paintings 89
palaces 8
Parliament 8, 23, 55, 59, 60, 61, 67, 69, 70, 71, 87, 91
Parr, Catherine 21
Pepys, Samuel 76
Philip, King of Spain 38, 42, 44, 48
plays 53
plumbing 12
Pope, the 9, 20, 21
Progresses 16–13

Protestants 9, 39, 42, 45, 83
Protestant country, England as a
    32, 43, 56, 59
Puritans 59, 60, 71, 84, 92

Raleigh, Sir Walter 47
Renaissance 52
Restoration 92
Richard III 14
roads 40, 62
Roundheads 69
royal court 8
Royal Mail 63
Royal Navy 26, 82
Royal Observatory, Greenwich
    77
Royal Society 76, 77
Rupert, Prince 68, 70

sailors 46, 47, 49, 79
St Paul's Cathedral 23, 79, 80
schools 23, 64
science 52, 76-7
Scotland 25, 44, 49, 54, 58, 61,
    74, 87, 91
Seymour, Jane 20
Shakespeare, William 53
ships 26, 47, 48, 49, 56
Simnel, Lambert 15
soldiers, Tudor 28-9
Somerset, Duke of 32
Spain 38-9
sport 16-17, 88
stocks 57
streets 31, 81
Stuarts
    Anne 82, 90-91
    Charles I 63, 66-8
    Charles II 74-8, 82
    James II 82-3, 86-7
    James VI of Scotland and I of
        England 54-9, 61

Oliver Cromwell 70-71, 74,
    75, 92
William III and Mary II 83,
    87, 90

tableware 37
tapestries 52
teeth 37
theatres, Stuart 71, 92-3
theatres, Tudor 53, 92
tobacco 17, 47
Tower of London 29
towns 30, 31, 63, 64, 81
trade 56, 70
travel, Stuart 62-3
travel, Tudor 40-41
travellers 23
Tudors
    Edward VI 20, 32-3
    Elizabeth I 13, 17, 20, 42-5,
        47, 54, 58
    Henry VII 9, 14-15, 44, 46
    Henry VIII 18-26, 32, 52
    Mary I 20, 32, 38-9, 42
Tyndale, William 33

Wales 24
Warbeck, Perkin 15
War of the Roses 14
wattle 30
weapons 28-9
weavers 43
William III and Mary II 83,
    86-7, 90
windows 31
witchcraft 57
Wolsey, Cardinal 19, 21
wool, 24, 56
work 16
Wren, Sir Christopher 80, 86
Wyatt, Sir Thomas 39

yeoman of the guard 29